# Etched by Silence

SWALLOW

# Etched by Silence

*A pilgrimage through the poetry*
*of R.S. Thomas*

*Compiled by*

Jim Cotter

CANTERBURY
PRESS
Norwich

© Copyright in the poems: Kunjana Thomas

The poems in this book are taken from
R. S. Thomas, *Collected Later Poems 1988–2000* (Bloodaxe Books, 2004)
R. S. Thomas, *Selected Poems 1946–1968* (Bloodaxe Books, 1986)
and are reproduced by kind permission of Bloodaxe Books.

© Copyright in the supplementary text
Jim Cotter, 2011 and 2013

© Copyright in the photographs
Susan Blagden, 2013

© Copyright in bird drawings and map
Ann Bewick

First published in the UK in 2011 by The Parochial Church Council,
St Hywyn's Church, Aberdaron, North Wales
www.st-hywyn.org.uk

Published by the Canterbury Press in 2013
Editorial office
Invicta House, 108–114 Golden Lane
London, EC1Y 0TG

Canterbury Press is an imprint of Hymns Ancient and Modern Ltd
(a registered charity)
13a Hellesdon Park Road, Norwich, Norfolk, NR6 5DR

www.canterburypress.co.uk

British Library Cataloguing in Publication data

A catalogue record for this book is available from the British Library

ISBN 978 1 84825 339 1

Typeset by Regent Typesetting, London
Printed and bound by
CPI Group (UK) Ltd, Croydon

# DEDICATION

*We pause upon the path:*
*the journey takes its toll:*
*we seek the Living Mystery,*
*the Way, the Heart, the Goal.*

*We fall in silence deep*
*and listen with intent:*
*no easy word comes from the sky:*
*is Nothing All that's meant?*

*We wait, alert and still,*
*and watch with spyglass trained:*
*a bird alights? a fleeting glance?*
*a sighting lost or gained?*

*O absent, puzzling Thou,*
*so far beyond our grasp,*
*a glorious empty breathing space*
*where we are found at last.*

*You play at hide and seek*
*when night displaces day:*
*we might have glimpsed a curtain twitch:*
*you give yourself away.*

BLACKBIRD

# CONTENTS

# PREFACE TO THE SECOND EDITION

LITTLE OWL

This short additional preface is being written a few weeks before the centenary of R.S.Thomas's birth on 29 March 1913. His reputation as a poet has of course been international for a generation or more, even if heart and soul he belongs to the Llŷn Peninsula of North Wales more than to anywhere else. It feels fitting that the first edition of this book was homemade within the parish of Aberdaron, and was printed near the road out of Porthmadog that leads the pilgrim westwards along the peninsula. It also feels fitting that this second edition has an international readership in mind. This has led to the only significant change: the suggestions in the top right hand corner of each double spread (each poem has its own two pages) still include locations that are specific to the Llŷn and Aberdaron, especially when it is clear that the poem has been inspired by an exact spot, but on the whole the reader is invited to imagine similar settings, either from memories or photographs. When you live by the sea it is easy to forget that there are millions of people in the world who have never set eyes on the ocean, indeed living thousands of miles from the sound of waves.

The compiler wants to add two acknowledgments to those listed in the original preface (which follows this one): he is grateful to Christine Smith and her colleagues at the Canterbury Press for enabling this book to travel more widely than it would otherwise have done, and to Kunjana and Gwydion Thomas and Bloodaxe Books for waiving copyright fees so that royalties can further the work of St Hywyn's Church, Aberdaron.

Lastly, a DVD was issued as a companion to the book when it was published in 2011. About half of the poems have been used in the recording, along with the filming of the landscapes and seascapes, produced in such a way that words and pictures feed each other, the whole being paced as an exercise in leisurely reflection. The DVD is still available. If you would like a copy, please email the compiler, jim@cottercairns.co.uk, and he will do his best to make sure it is sent on its way speedily.

Jim Cotter
*Aberdaron*
*March 2013*

*PREFACE*

Byron Rogers' biography of R.S.Thomas calls him 'the man who went into the west'. Indeed, in his adult life that is what he did, ministering in successive parishes in Wales before he reached the last village before Ireland, Aberdaron. As you travel down the Llŷn Peninsula, the land becomes more stark, swept clear of clutter, narrowing to the headlands at the tip where the sea takes over completely. The poems and the views begin to resonate with each other – not all of them of course, but sufficient for a pilgrim soul to explore the questions that arise from both the poetry and the landscape.

CHOUGH

Each poem in this selection had to have the answer Yes to three questions: It might not have been, but *could* it have been written in or around Aberdaron? Is it short enough to fit on one page of this book? Is it accessible enough on first reading? And the total number decided upon is 52, so that a leisurely pilgrimage in the imagination could be undertaken, one poem a week for a year. Perhaps most people, however, who chance upon this book will want to use it during a few days' visit, wandering and pondering – and probably needing an Ordnance Survey map to find the exact locations mentioned, and the roads and paths leading to them.

Each double page spread in the book has the poem top left, its source bottom left, a location for reading it top right, and a reflection by the compiler bottom right.

This leaves some space for the pilgrim to make his or her contribution to the conversation already going on between the poet, the compiler, and the landscape: there's room for another poem, or a drawing, or for pasting a photograph. If you let the landscape of Pen Llŷn, Aberdaron, and Ynys Enlli, Bardsey Island, speak to you, you may well find it questions you. So does the poet.

There are few poets who ask as many questions as R.S.Thomas does. They invite us to explore, and to take to mind and heart that which has no easy answers, and often remains unanswerable. And as counterpoint at the end of the book is a selection of questions from the Gospels. May your pilgrimage be blessed. This is not an easy book, nor an easy landscape, nor an easy poet, but they are in the end benign.

These words of John Pikoulis in the *New Welsh Review* are thought-provoking: 'Thomas's poems leave us chilled, yet oddly consoled. They reveal tremendous things to us but beyond them there is no further disappointment. At that point, the notion of disappointment itself founders.'

There are a few odd punctuation marks in the poems, and some slightly rarefied grammar, which may or may not be errors in the originals, but as far as the compiler is aware, after checking, the reprinting here is consistent with the two books of collected poems.

The compiler is grateful to the Parochial Church Council of Eglwys Sant Hywyn, Aberdaron, and Eglwys Sant Maelrhys, Llanfaelrhys, for their encouragement and support for this project, and in particular to the following people for their comments and for their help in proof-reading: Val Wood of Uwchmynydd, Lesley Wasley of High Wycombe, Andrew Sully of Llangollen, Verena Schiller of Aberdaron, David Marshallsay of Carreg, Aled Jones-Williams of Cricieth, Carol Friggins of Rhiw, and Marjorie Bates of Sheffield.

He is grateful also to Gwydion and Kunjana Thomas of Rhiw for permission to reprint the poems, to Susan Blagden of Bangor-is-y-Coed for the photographs, and to Ann Bewick of Anelog for the map and the drawings.

Writing this Preface near the sea in Aberdaron and about to release this book into the world, I'm even more than usually aware of the prayer of the Breton fisherman: 'Seigneur, votre mer est si grande, et ma barque est si petite.' This is a book of grand themes, vast seascapes, mysterious divinity, and questioning humanity.

Jim Cotter
*Aberdaron*
*March 2011*

There are other pilgrimages
    to make beside Jerusalem, Rome;
beside the one into the no-man's-
    land beyond the microscope's carry.
If you came in winter,
    you would find the tree
with your belief still crucified
    upon it, that for her at all

times was in blossom, the resurrection
    of one that had come seminally
down to raise the deciduous human
    body to the condition of his body.

From 'Fugue for Ann Griffiths',
*Welsh airs*, 1987

STONECHAT

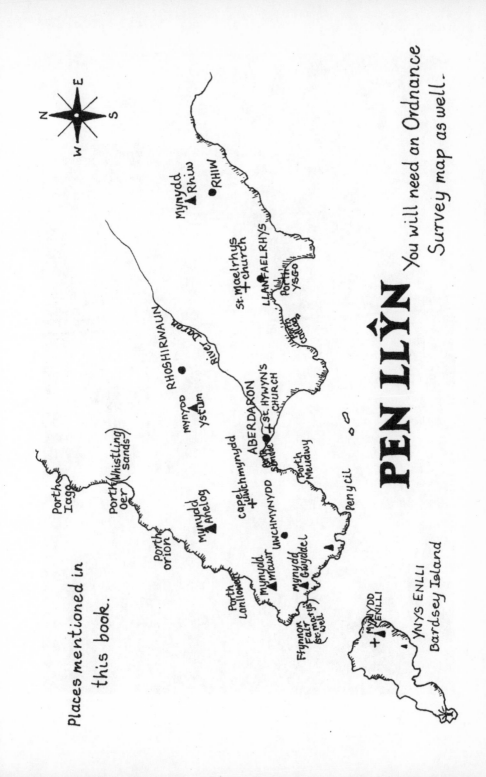

Places mentioned in this book.

# PEN LLŶN

You will need an Ordnance Survey map as well.

Porth Iago

Porth (Whistling
Oer Sands?)

Porth
orion

Mynydd
Anelog

Porth
Llanllawen

Mynydd
Mawr

Mynydd
Gwyddel

Flynnon
Fair
(st. mary's
well)

MYNYDD
ENLLI

YNYS ENLLI
Bardsey Island

capel mynydd

UWCHMYNYDD

Pen y cil

Porth
Meudwy

Porth
simdde

ST. HYWYN'S
CHURCH

ABERDARON

Mynydd
Ystum

RHOSHIRWAUN

River Daron

St. maelrhys
church

LLANFAELRHYS

Porth
Ysgo

Porth
Cadlan

Mynydd
Rhiw

RHIW

# THE POEMS

## One

## *Resolution*

The new year brings the old resolve
to be brave, to be patient,
to suffer the betrayal of birth
without flinching, without bitter
words. The way in was hard;
the way out could be made
easy, but one must not take
it; must await decay perhaps
of the mind, certainly of the mind's
image of itself that it has
projected. The bone aches, the blood
limps like a cripple about the ruins
of one's body. Yet what are these
but the infirmities that we share
with the creatures? It is the memories
that one has, the impenitent bungler
of love, refusing for too long
to say 'yes' to that earlier gesture
of love that had brought one
forth; it is these, as they grow
clearer with the telescoping
of the years, that constitute
for the beholder the true human pain.

From *The way of it*, 1977
*Collected poems,* p.309

Pausing at a boundary, a frontier, looking back to the territory that is familiar and looking forward into territory as yet unknown, and recognizing that you can never go back, only forward.

It is early, in the morning, in the year, a time for setting out: with resolve on a pilgrim journey, expecting no comforts, knowing that truth, to do its cleansing work, needs to be astringent, eyes and ears expectant, but without the expectation that keeps its eye so fixed on the destination that something unexpected, slanting into sight from the side of the path, is missed.

## Two

### The absence

It is this great absence
that is like a presence, that compels
me to address it without hope
of a reply. It is a room I enter

from which someone has just
gone, the vestibule for the arrival
of one who has not yet come.
I modernise the anachronism

of my language, but he is no more here
than before. Genes and molecules
have no more power to call
him up than the incense of the Hebrews

at their altars. My equations fail
as my words do. What resource have I
other than the emptiness without him of my whole
being, a vacuum he may not abhor?

From *Frequencies*, 1978
*Collected poems*, p.361

Looking round a room or house that you
have lived in, but is now empty. Furniture
and belongings have been packed and are in
a van outside.

Putting aside noise, information, meetings,
chatter, possessions, mobile phones ... step-
ping into the emptiness that is at the heart
of religion and science ... looking out on to
a vast space, empty of features, a moor or a
fen or a desert, and at the end of Pen Llŷn
an ocean or a black beclouded night sky.

**Three**

**The chapel**

A little aside from the main road,
becalmed in a last-century greyness,
there is the chapel, ugly, without the appeal
to the tourist to stop his car
and visit it. The traffic goes by,
and the river goes by, and quick shadows
of clouds, too, and the chapel settles
a little deeper into the grass.

But here once on an evening like this,
in the darkness that was about
his hearers, a preacher caught fire
and burned steadily before them
with a strange light, so that they saw
the splendour of the barren mountains
about them and sang their amens
fiercely, narrow but saved
in a way that men are not now.

From *Laboratories of the spirit*, 1975
*Collected poems*, p.276

Passing by a chapel that is now for sale or visiting a redundant church that has been stripped of its furnishings. (30 years before R.S. Thomas became Vicar of Aberdaron the 11 chapels within the parish/community boundary were thriving; 30 years after he left, only four still held services, none weekly, and there were no members under 70. But the buildings still dot the landscape, and the visitor won't have far to look to find one.)

The fire that warmed us flickers, embers cool. A few remain faithful, ageing, gathering less frequently than they did. Will the next generation's remnant keep them going? Chapels and churches: Philip Larkin called them serious places on serious earth. Who has the resolve to stay there, in prayer, in song, in word?

## Four

### The empty church

They laid this stone trap
for him, enticing him with candles,
as though he would come like some huge moth
out of the darkness to beat there.
Ah, he had burned himself
before in the human flame
and escaped, leaving the reason
torn. He will not come any more

to our lure. Why, then, do I kneel still
striking my prayers on a stone
heart? Is it in hope one
of them will ignite yet and throw
on its illumined walls the shadow
of someone greater than I can understand?

From *Frequencies*, 1978
*Collected poems*, p.349

Entering a church when nobody else is there, and standing still. Perhaps you will need to borrow the key. If so, lock yourself in for a few minutes. (R.S. Thomas may well have composed this poem in St Hywyn's Church in Aberdaron or in St Maelrhys' Church in Llanfaelrhys. St Hywyn's is open 10-ish to dusk in the winter months, 10 to 6-ish the rest of the year; St Maelrhys' is open all the time between Easter and the end of October. Try visiting at night …)

If the words no longer catch fire in the chapels, neither do the actions in the churches. Hope hardly finds it easy to fend off despair. Prayers seem so often to be like the sparks that come from a lighter that has no fuel for a flame. Is the 'someone greater' hidden in the darkness? If, against all expect-ation, there is a flame, what shape might its shadow be?

*Five*

*In church*

Often I try
to analyse the quality
of its silences. Is this where God hides
from my searching? I have stopped to listen,
after the few people have gone,
to the air recomposing itself
for vigil. It has waited like this
since the stones grouped themselves about it.
These are the hard ribs
of a body that our prayers have failed
to animate. Shadows advance
from their corners to take possession
of places the light held
for an hour. The bats resume
their business. The uneasiness of the pews
ceases. There is no other sound
in the darkness but the sound of a man
breathing, testing his faith
on emptiness, nailing his questions
one by one to an untenanted cross.

From *Pieta*, 1966
*Collected poems*, p180

Again going into a church when nobody else is there, and taking time to listen to the silence and asking what kind of silence?

A search, a silence, a vigil ... a hidden divinity ... lifeless stone, shadows, colonizing bats ... a man silent, questioning, with nothing but emptiness within the building and within himself ... breath the only sound where once there were words and music ...

## Six

### *The island*

And God said, I will build a church here
and cause this people to worship me,
and afflict them with poverty and sickness
in return for centuries of hard work
and patience. And its walls shall be hard as
their hearts, and its windows let in the light
grudgingly, as their minds do, and the priest's words
    be drowned
by the wind's caterwauling. All this I will do,

said God, and watch the bitterness in their eyes
grow, and their lips suppurate with
their prayers. And their women shall bring forth
on my altars, and I will choose the best
of them to be thrown back into the sea.

And that was only on one island.

From *H'm*, 1972
*Collected poems*, p.223

Looking at an old church in countryside whose soil has never been fertile and where the wind sweeps across the land. Imagine what it would have been like to live there 200 years ago. (This poem doesn't specifically mention Ynys Enlli, Bardsey Island, but it is probably the one that was in R.S. Thomas's mind when he wrote this poem. You can look across to the island from the end of the Llŷn Peninsula and you can also visit it for a day or stay there for a week, hoping for fair enough weather for the boat to be making the crossing.)

A centuries' old lament and complaint, but rarely expressed as bleakly and bitterly as it is here. The question raised does not of course go away. Pen Llŷn is a landscape for wrestling with it. The spirit of the place is benign, but does not let you get away with cheap and easy answers, such as religion sometimes peddles. The wind, the waves, the sharp light, scour.

**Seven**

**Pen Llŷn**

Dafydd looked out;
I look out: five centuries
without change? The same sea breaks
on the same shore and is not
broken. The stone in Llŷn
is still there, honey-
coloured for a girl's hair
to resemble. It is time's
smile on the cliff
face at the childishness
of my surprise. Here was the marriage
of land and sea, from whose bickering
the spray rises. 'Are you there?'
I call into the dumb
past, that is close to me
as my shadow. 'Are you here?'
I whisper to the encountered
self like one coming
on the truth asleep
and fearing to disturb it.

From *Mass for hard times*, 1992
*Collected later poems*, p.196

Bringing to mind a familiar beach, or, if you have always lived in the middle of a continent, a beach that you have seen on a film. (Within the parish of Aberdaron there are ten accessible beaches, five on the south coast, five on the north coast. Most involve at least a short walk from a car park. At Aberdaron itself the beach is but a few steps from the road.)

So often the perspective of time, what some call 'deep time', the scale of centuries, of geological eras, appears in these poems. To walk along the beach, to look at the folds of the rocks near Pen-y-Cil at the end of the peninsula, is to recognize this. The boundary between land and sea continually shifts, but it is always there. Land and sea endlessly clash, resonating with our questions, to and fro, between present and past, between surface self and deeper self, the latter so often asleep.

# Eight

## The porch

Do you want to know his name?
It is forgotten. Would you learn
What he was like? He was like
anyone else, a man with ears
and eyes. Be it sufficient
that in a church porch on an evening
in winter, the moon rising, the frost
sharp, he was driven
to his knees and for no reason
he knew. The cold came at him;
his breath was carved angularly
as the tombstones; an owl screamed.

He had no power to pray.
His back turned on the interior
he looked out on a universe
that was without knowledge
of him and kept his place
there for an hour on that lean
threshold, neither outside nor in.

From *Frequencies*, 1978
*Collected poems*, p.326

Imagining standing or sitting in a church gateway or porch and seeing there a wayfarer, or coffin bearers sheltering from the rain.

Spiritually speaking, porches are crowded places these days. So many people are not sure, half in, half out, as old forms of faith wither and new shoots begin to appear. We live not knowing if these are weeds or flowers. To change the metaphor, we may be feeling our way across a bridge in fog, not knowing if it touches the other side, not knowing what the other side will look like. We know only that we can't go back.

# Nine

### Poste Restante

I want you to know how it was,
whether the Cross grinds into dust
under men's wheels or shines brightly
as a monument to a new era.

There was a church and one man
served it, and few worshipped
there in the raw light on the hill
in winter, moving among the stones
fallen about them like the ruins
of a culture they were too weak
to replace, too poor themselves
to do anything but wait
for the ending of a life
they had not asked for.
                        The priest would come
and pull on the hoarse bell nobody
heard, and enter that place
of darkness, sour with the mould
of the years. And the spider would run
from the chalice, and the wine lie
there for a time, cold and unwanted
by all but he, while the candles
guttered as the wind picked
at the roof. And he would see
over that bare meal his face
staring at him from the cracked glass
of the window, with the lips moving
like those of an inhabitant of
a world beyond this.
                        And so back
to the damp vestry to the book
where he would scratch his name and the date
he could hardly remember, Sunday
by Sunday, while the place sank
to its knees and the earth turned
from season to season like the wheel
of a great foundry to produce
you, friend, who will know what happened.

From *Laboratories of the spirit*, 1975
*Collected poems*, p.272

Standing before a cross or crucifix, or hold-
ing a cross in your hand, or picturing a
crucifixion as an historical event, contem-
plating awhile this most familiar shape.
Bringing to mind the way in which buildings
– and forms of faith – flourish and decay.

And what *do* we make of the Cross? For
most people it is either a piece of jewel-
lery or a footnote to the history of barbaric
executions. To many a historian, it is the
last gasp of an impossible dream. To many
a theologian, an interpretation of 'appeas-
ing a wrathful father' in order to deflect his
fury from human beings, is an immoral relic
from a form of religion dominated by fear.
Does the cross on an altar have the power to
draw us close? If so, to what, to whom? Is
it untenanted, unoccupied? Or is this to be
faithless, unaware of a silent suffering pres-
ence closer than breathing?

## Ten

### *'But the silence in the mind'*

But the silence in the mind
is when we live best, within
listening distance of the silence
we call God. This is the deep
calling to deep of the psalm-
writer, the bottomless ocean
we launch an armada of
our thoughts on, never arriving.

It is a presence, then,
whose margins are our margins;
that calls us out over our
own fathoms. What to do
but draw a little nearer to
such ubiquity by remaining still?

From *Counterpoint*, 1990
*Collected Later Poems*, p.118

Going to or imagining a place where sea and land meet dramatically, with much to see and to hear. Becoming aware of the depths of the ocean and the expanse beyond the horizon.

It is that time on a journey, even on a walk with a friend, when we fall silent, putting the noise of words to one side, going deeper within, recognizing the questions that rise to the surface when we inhabit the margins, the places on the edge, the 'between' places, the threshold, in Welsh 'trothwy'. To become silent, to become still, is simple, but not easy: indispensable though.

**Eleven**

**Cones**

Simple in your designs,
infinite in your variations
upon them: the leaf's veins,
the shell's helix, the stars themselves
gyring down to a point
in the mind; the mind also
from that same point spiralling
outward to take in space.

Heartening that in our journeys
through time we come round not
to the same place, but recognize it
from a distance. It is the dream
we remember, that makes us say:
"We have been here before." In
truth we are as far from it
as one side of the cone
from the other, and in between
are the false starts, the failures,
the ruins from which we climbed,
not to look down, but to feel your glance
resting on us at the next angle
of the gyre.
              God, it is not your reflections
we seek, wonderful as they are
in the live fibre; it is the possibility
of your presence at the cone's
point towards which we soar
in hope to arrive at the still
centre, where love operates
on all those frequencies
that are set up by the spinning
of two minds, the one on the other.

From *Experimenting with an Amen*, 1986
*Collected poems*, p.478

Holding in your hand a spiral-shaped shell or picturing one in your mind, or the geometric image of a spiral, as in many Celtic designs.

The spiral may be the most evocative pattern in nature's geometry. When T.S.Eliot in *Four Quartets* wrote of our arriving where we started and knowing the place for the first time, was he thinking of a circle or of a spiral? And spiralling up or spiralling down? I have not had the patience to read through all R.S. Thomas's poems simply to find all the instances of the word 'love'. But I suspect there are more than his crusty reputation would lead many to think, and I also have a hunch that he uses the word more frequently in the second half of his composing days than in the first.

**Twelve**

**Ffynnon Fair**

They did not divine it, but
they bequeathed it to us:
clear water, brackish at times,
complicated by the white frosts
of the sea, but thawing quickly.

Ignoring my image, I peer down
to the quiet roots of it, where
the coins lie, the tarnished offerings
of the people to the pure spirit
that lives there, that has lived there
always, giving itself up
to the thirsty, withholding
itself from the superstition
of others, who ask for more.

From *Laboratories of the spirit*, 1975
*Collected poems*, p.292

This poem refers to St Mary's Well at the end of the Llŷn Peninsula. It can be reached by a footpath and a tricky scramble over rocks, and only at low tide. (Companion and care advised.) There are wells and fountains galore to choose from to picture in mind's eye, with many of them receiving coins.

In turbulent salt water fills the well, draining away as the tide ebbs, giving way to the fresh water that comes from underground. And you? Do you arrive physically thirsty on a rare hot day? Or aware of a thirst for living water? Or superstitious? Or simply curious? Or expectant ...?

## Thirteen

### Finality

Nose running, eyes running; time
running out. Too late
to be wise, may I be
intrepid. There is,
they say, between us
and the light, the dark
we must wander, seeking
for the self that was
allotted to us, which we refused.

Do we put too much
on? Is the self there
so pared down as to be
invisible as glass?
If not thin, then neither
am I a rich man.
Maybe I will slip through
the eye of the needle on which
the saved are to be threaded.

I have dismissed my camel,
dispensed with my car.
On foot now, too proud
despite it to hitch lifts,
I approach that cleft
where, as once I was squeezed
in, I will be squeezed out
into what I must confide
is the darkness of his shadow.

From *Residues*, 2002
*Collected later poems*, p.331

Visiting or imagining any 'land's end', with the sea impinging ever more emphatically, wind and currents in all directions, reaching the 'point' of no return and faced with the needle's eye that none can avoid. (The hill on Bardsey Island, Mynydd Enlli, has the shape of the eye of a needle: no wonder the old missionary-monks went there to die.)

Ronald Stuart and his first wife Mildred Elsi lived a life more spartan than most of us would now choose. The only sop to winter was a one-bar electric fire. And that raises questions for us on the journey. What do we need to do without so that we may grow within? Of what do we need to be dispossessed? Possessions? Words? Money? People? Do we live inside these statements? Enough is enough. We have enough. And maybe more than enough. Or are our physical or mental diminishments the route we have to take? Some witness to a beam of light leaping upwards from a body that has breathed out for the last time. Is our aim, through our dying, to be the crack of light between a door and a wall?

*Fourteen*

*Folk tale*

Prayers like gravel
        flung at the sky's
window, hoping to attract
        the loved one's
attention. But without
        visible plaits to let
down for the believer
        to climb up,
to what purpose open
        that far casement?
        I would
have refrained long since
        but that peering once
through my locked fingers
I thought that I detected
        the movement of a curtain.

From *Experimenting with an Amen*, 1986
*Collected poems*, p.517

Imagining – or remembering – your Romeo or Juliet moment, balancing gravel in your hand, throwing it at a window, wondering if it will be heard.

How long can a crumb sustain a body, how long can a glimpse sustain a faith? To crumble, to fade, is to become nothing. Faith is then the trust that something is created out of nothing. Let go ... Let be ... Let 'God' ...

## Fifteen

### Groping

Moving away is only to the boundaries
of the self. Better to stay here,
I said, leaving the horizons
clear. The best journey to make
is inward. It is the interior
that calls. Eliot heard it.
Wordsworth turned from the great hills
of the north to the precipice
of his own mind, and let himself
down for the poetry stranded
on the bare ledges.
      For some
it is all darkness; for me, too,
it is dark. But there are hands
there I can take, voices to hear
solider than the echoes
without. And sometimes a strange light
shines, purer than the moon,
casting no shadow, that is
the halo upon the bones
of the pioneers who died for truth.

From *Frequencies*, 1978
*Collected poems*, p.328

Visiting or thinking of a cliff, a quarry, a rock face in the mountains – or the edge of a mineshaft. Take care, stand still, look.

Nothing coming over the horizon ... nothing coming from out there ... And from in here? Not before a perilous descent down a creaking rusty ladder that barely holds to the wall of a neglected mineshaft. And is the strange light Henry Vaughan's 'dazzling darkness'?

## Emerging

Not as in the old days I pray,
God. My life is not what it was.
Yours, too, accepts the presence of
the machine? Once I would have asked
healing. I go now to be doctored,
to drink sinlessly of the blood
of my brother, to lend my flesh
as manuscript of the great poem
of the scalpel. I would have knelt
long, wrestling with you, wearing
you down. Hear my prayer, Lord, hear
my prayer. As though you were deaf, myriads
of mortals have kept up their shrill
cry, explaining your silence by
their unfitness.
                It begins to appear
this is not what prayer is about.
It is the annihilation of difference,
the consciousness of myself in you,
of you in me; the emerging
from the adolescence of nature
into the adult geometry
of the mind. I begin to recognise
you anew, God of form and number.
There are questions we are the solution
to, others whose echoes we must expand
to contain. Circular as our way
is, it leads not back to that snake-haunted
garden, but onward to the tall city
of glass that is the laboratory of the spirit.

From *Laboratories of the spirit*, 1975
*Collected poems*, p.263

Holding in one hand a marvel of techno-
logical invention and in the other hand a
flower of intricate ingenuity, pondering what
kind of prayer comes to you as you look. An
experiment in contemplation. A laboratory
moment.

Are all desires childish? Do we transfer our
questions and hopes from God to surgeons?
Could you possibly say to the parents of a
child whose disability stems from a genetic
malfunction, If only you have more faith
the child would be cured? Do all our cries
vanish into nothing? Into emptiness? What
is prayer, for grown-ups?

**Seventeen**

*Island*

I would still go there
if only to await
the once-in-a-lifetime
opening of truth's flower;

if only to escape
such bought freedom, and live,
prisoner of the keyless sea,
on the mind's bread and water.

From *No truce with the Furies,* 1995
*Collected later poems,* p.283

Putting to one side the complexities of our
lives and simplifying them, focusing on a
flower, a piece of bread, and a glass of water.

One of a number of short, simple, limpid
poems that R.S. Thomas wrote towards
the end of his life. Perhaps we will become
content with the paring down to the bare
and the simple, with the illumination of a
rare moment, with the stripping away of the
delusion that we can buy freedom, and the
paradoxical consolation of being imprisoned
on the sea, with the most meagre of rations.

*Eighteen*

*Kneeling*

Moments of great calm,
kneeling before an altar
of wood in a stone church
in summer, waiting for the God
to speak; the air a staircase
for silence; the sun's light
ringing me, as though I acted
a great role. And the audiences
still; all that close throng
of spirits waiting, as I,
for the message.
                    Prompt me, God;
but not yet. When I speak,
though it be you who speak
through me, something is lost.
The meaning is in the waiting.

From *Not that he brought flowers*, 1968
*Collected poems*, p.199

Seeking out a place of utter stillness and silence: not easy in the city, not as easy as you might think in the countryside. Perhaps in the small hours. Perhaps in a crypt. Perhaps in a bathroom. Perhaps you'll have to hire a soundproofed studio and sleep there one night.

This poem, written a generation before the previous one, 'Island', nevertheless resonates with it. The simplicity again: the silence, the stillness, the waiting, which the visitor to this peninsula and island may hope once in a while to experience, T.S.Eliot's 'silence between two waves of the sea'. So hard, though, to wait and remain calm, and only then to discern the meaning ...

## Nineteen

### The letter

I look up from my book,
from the unreality of language,
and stare at the sea's surface
that says nothing and means it.

This morning there came this letter
from the heart's stranger, promising
to pray for me. What does that
mean? I, who am a man of prayer,

ask and am silent. Would he
make me insolvent? Strip me
of initiatives in order to repay
trust? Must I refrain from walking

this same sea, lest sinking
I should deride him? Operate
my vehicle at no speed
to attribute to him the safety

in which I arrive? I think his god
is not my god, or he would not
ask for such things. I admit
he has driven me to my knees

but with my eyes open so that,
by long looking over concealed
fathoms, I gaze myself into accepting
that to pray true is to say nothing.

From *Mass for hard times*, 1992
*Collected later poems*, p.201

Imagining you are looking out over the sea
from the same window every day – or what
it is like to be in the middle of the ocean out
of sight of land – or over a featureless moor
or a trackless desert.

The word 'nothing' appears in the first and
last stanza of this poem. The surface of the
sea says nothing. Is that marvellous? Or
does that speak of its indifference towards
us? And do we discover a freedom from the
tyranny of words when they no longer com-
municate. Can we be liberated by 'nothing'?
And what of the one who prays, even if still
kneeling, with eyes open, saying nothing?
Nothing as the gateway to true prayer? A
relief? A calm acceptance? Is that reflected
by King Lear's spiritual journey? Is his
tragic realization of 'never' redeemed by his
acceptance of being reduced to 'nothing'?

## Twenty

### Migrants

He is that great void
we must enter, calling
to one another on our way
in the direction from which
he blows. What matter
if we should never arrive
to breed or to winter
in the climate of our conception?

Enough we have been given wings
and a needle in the mind
to respond to his bleak north.
There are times even at the Pole
when he, too, pauses in his withdrawal,
so that it is light there all night long.

From *Mass for hard times*, 1992
*Collected later poems*, p.204

Watching the passing-by of a flock of birds migrating – or gathering in lines on telephone wires. (The end of the Llŷn Peninsula is a bird watcher's paradise, and there is a bird observatory and nature reserve on Ynys Enlli, Bardsey Island.) Picture, too, a magnet, or that invisible force that draws birds as well as iron filings. And how much daylight is there today and how gloomy or bright?

Consolation is hard won, astringent, nevertheless exhilarating. We move into emptiness, but we are still moving. For a time we lose all sense of direction, yet we may become aware of a magnet we did not know was within us. And the polar light might be sharper even than that of Pen Llŷn on a clear winter's day.

## Twenty-one

**Pilgrimages**

There is an island there is no going
to but in a small boat the way
the saints went, travelling the gallery
of the frightened faces of
the long-drowned, munching the gravel
of its beaches. So I have gone
up the salt lane to the building
with the stone altar and the candles
gone out, and kneeled and lifted
my eyes to the furious gargoyle
of the owl that is like a god
gone small and resentful. There
is no body in the stained window
of the sky now. Am I too late?
Were they too late also, those
first pilgrims? He is such a fast
God, always before us and
leaving as we arrive.
                    There are those here
not given to prayer, whose office
is the blank sea that they say daily.
What they listen to is not
hymns but the slow chemistry of the soil
that turns saints' bones to dust,
dust to an irritant of the nostril.

There is no time on this island.
The swinging pendulum of the tide
has no clock; the events
are dateless. These people are not
late or soon; they are just
here with only the one question
to ask, which life answers
by being in them. It is I
who ask. Was the pilgrimage
I made to come to my own
self, to learn that in times
like these and for one like me
God will never be plain and
out there, but dark rather and
inexplicable, as though he were in here?

From *Frequencies*, 1978
*Collected poems*, p.364

There is only one island that corresponds to the images of this poem, the ancient island of pilgrimage, Bardsey, Enlli. If you don't know it and you have access to the internet, you'll soon find photographs of the island. Lines four and five in the poem refer rather gruesomely to the pilgrims who were drowned while crossing the treacherous sound from the mainland. There are half a dozen criss-crossing surface currents and a similar number of up and down ones.

The island with the reputation as a place of pilgrimage, not as fearsome as Skellig Michael off the coast of Ireland, but not as easy to reach as Lindisfarne or Iona. And is the necessary journey now not to a place out there, but to an unknown destination deep within your being?

## Twenty-two

## *Sea-watching*

Grey waters, vast
    as an area of prayer
that one enters. Daily
    over a period of years
I have let the eye rest on them.
Was I waiting for something?
               Nothing
but that continuous waving
    that is without meaning
occurred.
      Ah, but a rare bird is
rare. It is when one is not looking,
at times one is not there
          that it comes.
You must wear your eyes out,
as others their knees.
     I became the hermit
of the rocks, habited with the wind
and the mist. There were days,
so beautiful the emptiness
it might have filled,
        its absence
was as its presence; not to be told
any more, so single my mind
after its long fast,
      my watching from praying.

From *Laboratories of the spirit*, 1975
*Collected poems*, p.306

Picturing the sea on a grey winter day, perhaps misty with the sound of a foghorn, perhaps rough with the sound of the wind. And imagine being given the sudden presence of a bird you cannot identify.

We do not often come across the idea, let alone the practice, of a fast of the *mind*. But that might be the way to clarity of thought and vision – and the moment of union, where absence and presence, emptiness and fulness are one. And until we have learned to wait and be still, that rare bird will not trust us enough to come near.

**Twenty-three**

*Swifts*

The swifts winnow the air.
It is pleasant at the end of the day
to watch them. I have shut the mind
on fools. The 'phone's frenzy
is over. There is only the swifts'
restlessness in the sky
and their shrill squealing.
                      Sometimes they glide
or rip the silk of the wind
in passing. Unseen ribbons
are trailing upon the air.
There is no solving the problem
they pose, that had millions of years
behind it, when the first thinker
looked at them.
                    Sometimes they meet
in the high air; what is engendered
at contact? I am learning to bring
only my wonder to the contemplation
of the geometry of their dark wings.

From *Pieta*, 1966
*Collected poems*, p.154

Next time you see a bird, stop, be still, look. Observe its movements. And return if you can the next day and stand in the same place. It may reveal itself again. Or the next day or ...

As so often, simple but difficult: looking, observing, giving attention, a reverence towards who or what is being contemplated, evoking wonder. Quieting the restless questioning mind.

## Twenty-four

### Tell us

We have had names for you:
the Thunderer, the Almighty
Hunter, Lord of the snowflake
and the sabre-toothed tiger.
One name we have held back
unable to reconcile it
with the mosquito, the tidal-wave,
the black hole into which
time will fall. You have answered
us with the image of yourself
on a hewn tree, suffering
injustice, pardoning it;
pointing as though in either
direction; horrifying us
with the possibility of dislocation.
Ah, love, with your arms out
wide, tell us how much more
they must still be stretched
to embrace a universe drawing
away from us at the speed of light.

From *Mass for hard times*, 1992
*Collected later poems*, p.170

Imagining a bare tree in winter, perhaps
split by lightning, stark against the sky.

There is no dodging the cross with R.S.
Thomas. All those names for God that are
power-as-might-and-violence are in endless
conversation with the suffering, the forgiv-
ing, the dislocation – and of course with an
understanding of the universe very differ-
ent from that of our ancestors. There is no
premature or easy Easter here, no straight-
forward resolution of the Good Friday ques-
tions.

## Twenty-five

## *Tidal*

The waves run up the shore
and fall back. I run
up the approaches of God
and fall back. The breakers return
reaching a little further,
gnawing away at the main land.
They have done this thousands
of years, exposing little by little
the rock under the soil's face.
I must imitate them only
in my return to the assault,
not in their violence. Dashing
my prayers at him will achieve
little other than the exposure
of the rock under his surface.
My returns must be made
on my knees. Let despair be known
as my ebb-tide; but let prayer
have its springs, too, brimming,
disarming him; discovering somewhere
among his fissures deposits of mercy
where trust may take root and grow.

From *Mass for hard times*, 1992
*Collected later poems*, p.167

Thinking about the erosion of a coast-line, perhaps now receding more quickly, the cliffs battered by the waves below and riven by rivulets in a time of flood and by landslides after a period of heavy rain. And imagine, revealed, a beautiful stone – or a plant finding at least temporary root in a newly formed hollow or cleft. (Stones falling on to the beach at Aberdaron have not seen the light of day since they were trapped in the earth in the Ice Age.)

The tide turns, hope returns. No violent rage spent, and an image in the last three lines worth letting take root in heart and inner eye.

## Twenty-six

## *Waiting*

Face to face? Ah, no
God; such language falsifies
the relation. Nor side by side,
nor near you, nor anywhere
in time and space.
                    Say you were,
when I came, your name
vouching for you, ubiquitous
in its explanations. The
earth bore and they reaped:
God, they said, looking
in your direction. The wind
changed; over the drowned
body it was you
they spat at.
                    Young
I pronounced you. Older
I still do, but seldomer
now, leaning far out
over an immense depth, letting
your name go and waiting,
somewhere between faith and doubt,
for the echoes of its arrival.

From *Frequencies*, 1978
*Collected poems*, p.347

Remembering yourself as a child leaning out over a rock to look into the depths of a pool? Or lying on the grass on a summer night and looking at the stars? Maybe there's time and opportunity to do that again. Or ask your grandchildren to do it and then come and tell you what they have seen.

Again, this stripping away of childhood's god, stranded as an idol, dead to our maturing selves. A corpse washed up on the shore deals the final blow. A reluctance now to utter a divine name, a shout sounding ridiculous and unnecessary, a whisper probably lost in the waves. And yet ...

## Twenty-seven

## *Threshold*

I emerge from the mind's
cave into the worse darkness
outside, where things pass and
the Lord is in none of them.

I have heard the still, small voice
and it was that of the bacteria
demolishing my cosmos. I
have lingered too long on

this threshold, but where can I go?
To look back is to lose the soul
I was leading upward towards
the light. To look forward? Ah,

what balance is needed at
the edges of such an abyss.
I am alone on the surface
of a turning planet. What

to do but, like Michelangelo's
Adam, put my hand
out into unknown space,
hoping for the reciprocating touch?

From *Between here and now*, 1981
Not printed in either *Collected poems* nor *Collected later poems*

If you've been in Rome and seen the Sistine Chapel – or you've seen the work of Michelangelo in a book – recall the figures painted there of the Creator and Adam. Or place the bowl of a stethoscope on your stomach and listen to the peristaltic movements making noises the ear cannot hear (many more and a greater variety than the rumbles you *can* hear).

The reference is to the story of Elijah in 1 Kings 19.11–12, with the 'storm-god' absent, present neither in the wind nor the earthquake nor the fire. Only then was there a 'still small voice', 'a sound of sheer silence'. Was this a moment of revelation in the evolution of human understanding of the divine? And for us? Are we at a new time of transition, as we contemplate bacteria and cosmos, and feel vertigo on the edge of an unfathomable chasm? The thought arises of the divine energy moving on a vast scale, yet known only as a fleeting touch. We live in a complex universe, ever ancient, ever new.

There are no easy answers. Perhaps as Rowan Williams put it in the New Welsh Review, for R.S. Thomas God is the one who enables us 'to ask the unanswerable questions'.

## Twenty-eight

### Andante

Masters, you who would initiate
me in discourse, apostrophising
the deity: O Thou, to Whom...
out of date three hundred
years. The atoms translate
into their own terms, burnishing
the dust, converting it
to a presence, a movement of light
on the room's wall, a smile quickening
and going out as the clouds
canter. Inhabitants of a flower
they fix that gaze on us
which is without focus, but compels
the attention, mesmerising us until
we are adrift on its scent's timelessness.
The huskiness of an emotion!
Can molecules feel? There is the long sigh
from the shore, the wave clearing
its throat to address us, requiring
no answer than the due
we give these things that share
the world with us, that compose
the world: an ever-renewed
symphony to be listened to
admiringly, even as we perform
it on whatever instruments
the generations put into our hands.

From *Experimenting with an Amen*, 1986
*Collected poems*, p.524

Looking at the dust in the air, seen in a beam of sunlight in a bedroom; listening to the sounds of the sea, perhaps mingling with the sounds of a river whose exit bisects a beach. And as a bonus playing a flute or a harp or a guitar or listening to a companion play.

What do we do now with our desires and requests and petitions? Is there not even a still small voice in reply? Is there only silence from heaven? Has the supernatural deity gone deaf? Do we have to move onwards, perhaps, to a mystical union where everything that we thought we lacked no longer impinges upon us?

There is among us a growing sense of the connectedness of all things, atoms and clouds, light and flowers, molecules and waves. With eyes open we see the instruments and the players, objects in front of us; and with eyes closed we hear only the waves of sound, only the music. But not one without the other.

Distinguishable but not separate. We simply have to give due attention to what is. And, in time, with the poet Rilke we shall have lived with the questions for so long that we shall have begun to learn how to live into the answers.

*Twenty-nine*

## Emerging

Well, I said, better to wait
for him on some peninsula
of the spirit. Surely for one
with patience he will happen by
once in a while. It was the heart
spoke. The mind, sceptical as always
of the anthropomorphisms
of the fancy, knew he must be put together
like a poem or a composition
in music, that what he conforms to
is art. A promontory is a bare
place; no God leans down
out of the air to take the hand
extended to him. The generations have
watched there
in vain. We are beginning to see
now it is matter is the scaffolding
of spirit; that the poem emerges
from morphemes and phonemes; that
as form in sculpture is the prisoner
of the hard rock, so in everyday life
it is the plain facts and natural happenings
that conceal God and reveal him to us
little by little under the mind's tooling.

From *Frequencies*, 1978
*Collected poems*, p.355

Standing on a cliff at the end of a peninsula; looking at the scaffolding supporting a building; thinking about how words come into being and take wing; looking at a half-finished sculpture, the figures still emerging from the stone.

Are we still waiting for a revelation in the old way, as for an old friend who may or may not turn up? Do we still yearn for a father who will make it all right? The mind finds that hard to believe in, even as a remote possibility. No, let the mind start with the wonder, intricacy, complexity of evolution and its mysterious sense of direction: the evidence of the 'plain facts' and the 'natural happenings', received and understood. Do we need now the authority of *evidence*?

## Thirty

### Nuance

With the cathedrals thundering
at him, history proving
him the two-faced god, there were
the few who waited on him
in the small hours, undaunted
by the absence of an echo
to their Amens. Physics' suggestion
is they were not wrong. Reality
is composed of waves and particles
coming at us as the Janus-faced
chooses. We must not despair.
The invisible is yet susceptible
of being inferred. To pray, perhaps, is
to have a part in an infinitesimal deflection.

From *No truce with the Furies*, 1995
*Collected later poems*, p.236

Walking round a cathedral; thinking about
matter and energy and the findings of
physics.

There is now evidence of the power of a
thought, both positive and negative. (Even
to be prayed for may not be benign: it can
feel being 'prayed at'…) There was a moun-
taineer who said that prayer for him was
aligning his will and energy, hardly of great
signficance in the grand scheme, with the
divine will and energy. Collaborating with
God as a junior partner?

# Thirty-one

## Nuclear

It is not that he can't speak;
who created languages
but God? Nor that he won't;
to say that is to imply
malice. It is just that
he doesn't, or does so at times
when we are not listening, in
ways we have yet to recognise

as speech. We call him the dumb
God with an effrontery beyond
pardon. Whose silence so eloquent
as his? What word so explosive
as that one Palestinian
word with the endlessness of its fall-out?

From *Laboratories of the spirit*, 1975
*Collected poems*, p.317

Imagining a silent place if you are in a noisy place, or a noisy place if you are in a silent place, and remembering pictures of a mushroom cloud.

R.S. Thomas's poems are like the Gospels, at least in this: they are full of questions. Is faith more a matter of living with questions than, perhaps, dying with answers – or other people dying because their answers are not yours? It is hard to think of two better questions than those at the end of this poem. I suspect that it is the first time that the impact of Jesus has been expressed in atomic imagery.

***Thirty-two***

***The other***

There are nights that are so still
that I can hear the small owl calling
far off and a fox barking
miles away. It is then that I lie
in the lean hours awake, listening
to the swell born somewhere in the Atlantic
rising and falling, rising and falling
wave on wave on the long shore
by the village, that is without light
and companionless. And the thought comes
of that other being who is awake, too,
letting our prayers break on him,
not like this for a few hours,
but for days, years, for eternity.

From *Destinations*, 1985
*Collected poems*, p.457

Also from *The echoes return slow*,1988
*Collected later poems*, p.51

Listening outside to the sounds of night; picturing and hearing the swell of the ocean and the waves coming towards a beach; walking by the sea in the darkness.

In the *Collected later poems* this one is preceded by a short paragraph: 'Minerva's bird, *Athene noctua*; too small for wisdom, yet unlike its tawnier cousin active by day, too, its cat's eyes bitterer than the gorse petals. But at night it was lyrical, its double note sounded under the stars in counterpoint to the fall of the waves.' There is perhaps another poem in that connection between cat's eyes and gorse petals through the word 'bitter'. It's very R.S. Thomas, as is the picture of prayers as waves falling relentlessly on God: elsewhere that kind of praying ceases, as, from time to time, do the waves and their sound, when the wind falls to calm.

**Thirty-three**

**Pre-Cambrian**

Here I think of the centuries,
six million of them, they say.
Yesterday a fine rain fell;
today the warmth has brought out the crowds.
After Christ, what? The molecules
are without redemption. My shadow
sunning itself on this stone
remembers the lava. Zeus looked down
on a brave world, but there was
no love there; the architecture
of their temples was less permanent
than these waves. Plato, Aristotle,
all those who furrowed the calmness
of their foreheads are responsible
for the bomb. I am charmed here
by the serenity of the reflections
in the sea's mirror. It is a window
as well. What I need
now is a faith to enable me to out-stare
the grinning faces of the inmates of its asylum,
the failed experiments God put away.

From *Frequencies*, 1978
*Collected poems*, p.339

Picturing a dramatic cliff face or mountain precipice where bare rock is exposed, with all its curves and slants; imagining the depth of rock beneath your feet. (At the end of the Llŷn Peninsula there are outcrops of the pre-Cambrian era, ancient indeed.)

Are the rocks and the molecules, the lava and the waves, all of them with a history almost inconceivably long, nevertheless not as indifferent and separate from us as we think? There is a verse from St John's Gospel, where the evangelist puts into the mouth of Jesus these words: 'I and the Father are one.' Perhaps we are being led now to add a parallel line: 'I and the universe are one.' The mystics – and now some of the cosmologists – would say so. Maybe 'failure' is not the only way of interpreting evolution's cul-de-sacs. Nor our own. And even R.S. Thomas does not seem to dismiss entirely the possibility of a faith that sees beyond such bleak necessity.

## Thirty-four

### 'Years are miles'

*One headland looks at another headland. What one sees must depend on where one stands, when one stands. There was sun where he stood. But on the pre-Cambrian rocks there was also his shadow, the locker without a key, where all men's questions are stored.*

Years are miles to be
travelled in memory
only. The children have vanished.
Here is what they saw

over the water: a beetling
headland under a smooth
sky with myself absent.
How shallow the minds

they played by! Not like mine
now, this dark pool I
lean over on that same
headland, knowing it wrinkled

by time's wind, putting my hand
down, groping with bleeding
fingers for truths too
frightening to be brought up.

From *The echoes return slow*, 1988
*Collected later poems*, p.47

Sitting by the side of a pool left by the ebbing tide, or by a mountain tarn reflecting the hills on a clear day, or by a loch where you can't help wondering if there might indeed be something monstrous deep down.

I wonder if the minds of children at play are always shallow? Do we not from our earliest years have memories – however much we have lost touch with them – of blissful union with all that is, as well as the darkness of birthrights betrayed, vulnerability trampled on, tenderness violated? The psychotherapeutic process challenges the inner pilgrim to face the fear of dark truths rising into the light. And in the poem of a life, the fear need not have the last word. True enough, though, that fingers bleed in the process.

## Thirty-five

### The promise

Promising myself before bedtime
to contend more urgently
with the problem. From nothing
nothing comes. Behind everything –
something, somebody? In the beginning
violence, the floor of the universe
littered with fragments. After
that enormous brawl, where
did the dove come from? From what
acorn mind these dark
boughs among which at night
thought loses its way back
to its dim sources, onward
to that illuminated citadel
that truth keeps? Light's distances
are without meaning and unreconciled
by the domestic. I pit my furniture
against the emptiness that is beyond
Antares, but the equation
is not in balance. There are no cushions
for the emotions. Thermodynamic
cold or else incineration
of the planet – either way
there is no hope for the species.
Are Sophocles and Mozart sufficient
justification for the failure
to find out? Beyond
the stars are more stars where love, perhaps,
or intellect or the anonymous is busy.

From *No truce with the furies*, 1995
*Collected later poems*, p.263

Imagining a place where you can see far into the distance – ocean, moor, desert – or a place so dark that you can look at the sky's dome, anywhere that reminds you of the vastness of space and the aeons of time.

I smile at the Big Bang being likened to a 'brawl'. Might it not also be described as the Great Radiance? Again, the hint of the mystic's paradox of 'nothing' and 'all'. Blink once and there's nothing. Blink again and there's everything. And anyone who puts Mozart in the scales has my vote for the proposition that 'all' is not an accident and 'nothing' is the necessary condition for the endlessly evolving creativity of everything – even to the stars beyond our own night vision to where perhaps 'love … or intellect or the anonymous is busy.'

## Thirty-six

*Alive*

It is alive. It is you,
God. Looking out I can see
no death. The earth moves, the
sea moves, the wind goes
on its exuberant
journeys. Many creatures
reflect you, the flowers
your colour, the tides the precision
of your calculations. There
is nothing too ample
for you to overflow, nothing
so small that your workmanship
is not revealed. I listen
and it is you speaking.
I find the place where you lay
warm. At night, if I waken,
there are the sleepless conurbations
of the stars. The darkness
is the deepening shadow
of your presence; the silence a
process in the metabolism
of the being of love.

From *Laboratories of the spirit*, 1975
*Collected poems*, p.296

Experiencing a breezy day with clouds scudding, branches bending, flowers waving, animals moving, yourself walking.

R.S. Thomas? Yes – in exuberant mood ... the divine and the human intimately bound up with the whole universe ... the revelations of the telescope and the microscope, wonder at every scale, and the darkness 'the deepening shadow of your presence'... the text of this other book of Revelation written in the script of science.

I wonder if one of his secrets was that once in a while, on one of his nocturnal walks, he danced ... Surprised – perhaps once – by joy?

### Thirty-seven

### The bright field

I have seen the sun break through
to illuminate a small field
for a while, and gone my way
and forgotten it. But that was the pearl
of great price, the one field that had
the treasure in it. I realize now
that I must give all that I have
to possess it. Life is not hurrying

on to a receding future, nor hankering after
an imagined past. It is the turning
aside like Moses to the miracle
of the lit bush, to a brightness
that seemed as transitory as your youth
once, but is the eternity that awaits you.

From *Laboratories of the spirit*, 1975
*Collected poems*, p.302

Being alert to a weather forecast that expects 'sunny intervals' and to a viewpoint where you can survey the moving shadows and the shafts of sunlight.

The pearl of great price is of no worldly use. You might be able to sell it, but if you do it is no longer yours. In itself, it is simply priceless. All you can do is to give everything for it, to appreciate it for a moment or two in time, and then hand it on. So too is the burning bush, an eternal moment which you can't hold on to.

## Thirty-eight

## The Kingdom

It's a long way off but inside it
there are quite different things going on:
festivals at which the poor man
is king and the consumptive is
healed; mirrors in which the blind look
at themselves and love looks at them
back; and industry is for mending
the bent bones and the minds fractured
by life. It's a long way off, but to get
there takes no time and admission
is free, if you will purge yourself
of desire, and present yourself with
your need only and the simple offering
of your faith, green as a leaf.

From *H'm*, 1972
*Collected poems*, p.233

Looking at a green leaf in the first flush of summer.

A kingdom where 'the poor man is king.' If so, either the man ceases to be poor or the organization known as a kingdom implodes, for no worldly kingdom can operate from poverty at the centre. A deceptively simple poem, full of the paradoxes that are at the heart of the Gospel. Among R.S.Thomas's poems this is one of the most cheerful. But love does have a habit of slipping through the cracks in even the most forbidding of faces.

### Thirty-nine

### 'You show me two faces'

You show me two faces,
that of a flower opening
and of a fist contracting
like the gripping of ice.

You speak to me with two
voices, one thundering
on the ear's drum, the other
one mistakeable for silence.

Father, I said, domesticating
an enigma; and as though
to humour me you came.
But there are precipices

within you. Mild and dire,
now and absent, like us but
wholly other – which side
of you am I to believe?

From 'AD' *in Counterpoint* 1990
*Collected later poems*, p.121

Picturing a fist next to a flower, a still field bordering a fast stream, solid rock facing down crashing waves.

This to-ing and fro-ing in the paradoxes of faith and doubt: it's easy to waste energy lamenting the lack of resolution; better, if more difficult, to accept the endless movement, to observe oneself moving, not forgetting to smile, not taking oneself too seriously.

And this poem reminds me of the spiritual exercise of slowly opening and closing my fist, between welcoming what is coming to me and resisting what is coming.

As ever, the relentless paring away of the one-sided and the comfortable. Even to address God as Father, as the Lord's Prayer does, is 'to domesticate an enigma'. We can't stay for long with 'The bright field' and 'The kingdom'. Rested, refreshed, we continue the journey, with uncountable miles before us.

**Forty**

*'It was arranged so'*

It was arranged so:
An impression of nearness
contradicted by blank space.
An apparition in a tree
as of a face watching us,
changing to bark as we looked
close. For a being so large
to play hide and seek! Yet the air
drew an invisible curtain
between us and him. Coming
on his footprint in the snow
of our thought we had nothing
to measure its size by. We were
the thermometer and the barometer
of his weather, but approximate
only; what instrument could record
the pressure on us to disbelieve
when he turned cold? There were times
when, bending close over a flower,
thinking to penetrate the transparence
of its expression, we lost our footing
and fell into a presence illimitable
as its absence, descending motionlessly
in space-time, not into darkness
but into the luminosity of his shadow.

From 'AD' in *Counterpoint*, 1990
*Collected later poems*, p.116

Looking at flowers and how they are ar-
ranged in a hedge, looking at a footprint pre-
cise in the snow, tracing the shapes between
the bare branches of a tree, allowing oneself
to fall into whatever is simply there in front
of us.

This poem encourages me to 'play hide and
seek' with changing shapes and weather, to
be prepared to stop and be still as the eye
catches something it had almost missed. And
a 'fall', a 'descent', may have its shadow, but
in the game of 'hide and seek' even shadows
may prove to be illuminating ...

*Forty-one*

*The moon in Llŷn*

The last quarter of the moon
of Jesus gives way
to the dark; the serpent
digests the egg. Here
on my knees in this stone
church, that is full only
of the silent congregation
of shadows and the sea's
sound, it is easy to believe
Yeats was right. Just as though
choirs had not sung, shells
have swallowed them; the tide laps
at the Bible; the bell fetches
no people to the brittle miracle
of the bread. The sand is waiting
for the running back of the grains
in the wall into its blond
glass. Religion is over,
and what will emerge from the body
of the new moon, no one
can say.
            But a voice sounds
in my ear: Why so fast,
mortal? These very seas
are baptized. The parish
has a saint's name time cannot
unfrock. In cities that
have outgrown their promise people
are becoming pilgrims
again, if not to this place,
then to the recreation of it
in their own spirits. You must remain
kneeling. Even as this moon
making its way through the earth's
cumbersome shadow, prayer, too,
has its phases.

From *Laboratories of the spirit*, 1975
*Collected poems*, p.282

Imagining being in a church within sight and sound of the sea – or being a pilgrim journeying to a place of prayer, famous or obscure, in a city square or up an alleyway, standing foursquare against the wind or almost invisible by a farmyard, or any other pilgrim place that without your fully understanding why, draws you to it.

I am not quite sure which lines of W.B. Yeats the poet is referring to here, but my mind immediately goes to these, from 'The Second Coming', 1921:

... things fall apart, the centre cannot hold; mere anarchy is loosed upon the world ... the best lack all conviction, while the worst are full of passionate intensity.

And I don't think that 'cities have outgrown their promise', if only because of the pilgrim souls who live in them and find in their explorations plenty of opportunity for learning the lessons of pilgrimage. But I love this poem: it resonates deeply with the spirit of the place, Aberdaron, church, village, and parish.

**Forty-two**

**Raptor**

You have made God small,
setting him astride
a pipette or a retort
studying the bubbles,
absorbed in an experiment
that will come to nothing.

I think of him rather
as an enormous owl
abroad in the shadows,
brushing me sometimes
with his wing so the blood
in my veins freezes, able

to find his way from one
soul to another because
he can see in the dark.
I have heard him crooning
to himself, so that almost
I could believe in angels,

those feathered overtones
in love's rafters, I have heard
him scream, too, fastening
his talons in his great
adversary, or in some lesser
denizen, maybe, like you or me.

From *No truce with the Furies,* 1995
*Collected later poems,* p.256

Recalling the hoot of an owl or hearing one
as you walk the dog late in the evening; re-
calling the sight of a raptor swooping on its
prey.

Rowan Williams in his appreciation of
R.S.Thomas in the New Welsh Review
highlights the first three lines and the last
word of the second stanza, followed by the
first three lines of the third. I wonder if
he would blanch, as I do somewhat, at the
image of the talons fastened on me. Can
love be that fierce and even terrifying? I'm
reminded again of T.S.Eliot in *Four Quartets*,
in 'Little Gidding': we are redeemed from
fire by fire ...

✝

## Forty-three

*'That there ...'*

That there is the unfamiliar
too. That there is a landscape
that will through all time
resist our endeavours
at domestication. There is one
who models his disguises
without a thought, to whom
invisibility is as natural
as it is to be above
or below sound. He hides himself
in a seed so that exploding
silently he pervades the world.
He is the wilderness imprisoned
under our flagstones yet escaping
from them in a haemorrhage
of raw flowers. He bares his teeth
in the lightning, delivering
his electric bite, appals us
with his thunder only to unnerve us
further with the blessing of his held breath.

From *Residues*, 2002
*Collected later poems*, p.344

86

Standing in a city square or sitting in a room and imagining the wilderness beneath the paving stones or the floorboards; recalling the sound of thunder and the flash of lightning; then, after a pause to let the mind settle, catching the softest and quietest of breaths.

I can never think that R.S.Thomas, from pictures of him and from stories about him, was ever a 'domesticated' man, so much did he exult in wild places and a wild God, neither under human control. Yet he is also aware of the stillness in the eye of the storm, the blessing of 'his *held* breath', an image unexpected at the end of this poem, and unexpected to those schooled in the image of the Spirit as breath and wind, always active. Paradoxes again, not to be perplexed by, but to be stirred by, for our relishing and our laughter.

## Forty-four

### Praise

I praise you because
you are artist and scientist
in one. When I am somewhat
fearful of your power,
your ability to work miracles
with a set-square, I hear
you murmuring to yourself
in a notation Beethoven
dreamed of but never achieved.
You run off your scales of
rain water and sea water, play
the chords of the morning
and evening light, sculpture
with shadow, join together leaf
by leaf, when spring
comes, the stanzas of
an immense poem. You speak
all languages and none,
answering our most complex
prayers with the simplicity
of a flower, confronting
us, when we would domesticate you
to our uses, with the rioting
viruses under our lens.

From *Laboratories of the spirit*, 1975
*Collected poems*, p.318

Imagining people in your neighbourhood or city who are artists and scientists, poets and musicians, in studios and laboratories, in cafes and pubs, painting and researching, scribbling and composing: imagining the ferment – *and* the viruses and cancers that are *rioting.*

As in the previous poem, an unexpected and breath*taking* image at the end, after the delight and play of much of the rest of the poem.

## Forty-five

### 'I look out over the timeless sea'

I look out over the timeless sea
over the head of one, calendar
to time's passing, who is now open
at the last month, her hair wintry.

Am I catalyst of her mettle that,
at my approach, her grimace of pain
turns to a smile? What it is saying is:
"Over love's depths only the surface is wrinkled."

From *Counterpoint*, 1990
*Collected later poems*, p.72

The poem is counterpointed with these lines of prose:
   'Both female. Both luring us on, staring crystal-eyed over their unstable fathoms. After a lifetime's apprenticeship in navigating their surfaces, nothing to hope for but that for the love of both of them he would be forgiven.'

Picturing a well-known and well-loved face, lined and lived in. (R.S.Thomas's first wife, Mildred Elsi Eldridge, a considerable artist, is buried in the churchyard at Llanfaelrhys, a little under three miles east of Aberdaron.)

This is one of his later poems that are about married love, all luminous and limpid, though counterpointed by solitary journeys, both inner and outer, not finding it easy to learn the lessons of love.

Perhaps pilgrim and hermit souls never do. I am reminded of Laurens van der Post somewhere musing on how many people in the 20th century lived alone, that there was room in this world only for hermits, or at most hermits in pairs.

## Forty-six

### Retired

Not to worry myself any more
if I am out of step, fallen behind.
Let the space probes continue;
I have a different distance to travel.

Here I can watch the night sky,
listen to how one grass blade
grates on another as member
of a disdained orchestra.

There are no meetings to attend
now other than those nocturnal
gatherings, whose luminaries
fell silent millennia ago.

No longer guilty of wasting
my time, I take my place
by a lily-flower, believing
with Blake that when God comes

he comes sometimes by way
of the nostril. My failure, perhaps,
was to have had no sense of smell
for the holiness suspiring from forked humans.

I count over the hours put by
for repentance, pulling thought's buildings
down to make way for the new,
fooling myself with the assurance

that when he occurs it is as the weather
of prayer's forecast, never with all
the unexpectedness of his body's
lightning, naked upon a cross.

From *Mass for hard times*, 1992
*Collected later poems*, p.147

Relishing the wherever and whatever of the present moment, becoming idle, waiting, attending to a flower or a wound, taking time to notice what has been missed because of hurry and distraction.

Such a relief not to have to try and keep up with the latest technology or the latest messages received by the Hubble telescope. The pilgrim journey changes: there is 'a different distance to travel'. Not so much the outer journey, but the inner one, noticing what we hurried by, grass, stars, flowers – and humans who had been too easily dismissed. And there is still the need to be alert to delusions: R.S. wrote no poem saying that life or faith could ever be easy or cheap.

## Forty-seven

### 'Still going'

Still going;
eighty odd years,
no grumbling.
Smoked, drank, ate

what I liked. Did
as the blood
told me. Ironed
my will on a hard

board. Complaints?
They were common:
coughs, colds, changeableness
of the heart's

weather. Took the
wet with the dry.
Chewing as much
as I bit off,

sparing the mind
its dyspepsia. Will
there be mutiny
at the day's end? The spirit

retains its poise,
ready at any time now
for walking the bone's
plank over the dark waters.

From *Counterpoint*, 1990
*Collected later poems*, p.59

The poem is counterpointed by these words of
prose:
    'They were among Chaucer's pilgrims, but
journeying towards no Canterbury. They were
part of that great multitude which no man can
number, but not in white clothes. They were
not to be judged by him. Is there a judgment?
They were part of 'life's own self-delight' from
which had sprung 'the abounding, glittering
jet.'

Taking a last step, putting a full stop at the end of the last exam question you will ever answer, finishing a long walk to the end of a peninsula, knowing that another step would pitch you over the cliff, inhabiting a place of no return.

John Pikoulis in the New Welsh Review writes of R.S.Thomas as 'a sentinel who did duty for us in the abyss …'

Perhaps in his later years he was no longer trapped in the abyss: after all he did retire, he was occasionally seen to smile in public, and his early bleakness was sometimes warmed into gentle life. But he was never tempted by the sentimental or false, and this poem resonates with the previous one, suddenly jolting us out of the everyday incidents of old age.

## Forty-eight

### At the end

Few possessions: a chair,
a table, a bed
to say my prayers by,
and, gathered from the shore,
the bone-like, crossed sticks
proving that nature
acknowledges the Crucifixion.
All night I am at
a window not too small
to be frame to the stars
that are no further off
than the city lights
I have rejected. By day
the passers-by, who are not
pilgrims, stare through the rain's
bars, seeing me as prisoner
of the one view, I who
have been made free
by the tide's pendulum truth
that the heart that is low now
will be at the full tomorrow.

From *No truce with the Furies*, 1995
*Collected later poems*, p.246

Looking out of a window at what has become familiar to the eye, perhaps for decades, and, wherever you may be geographically, 'hearing' the constant flow and ebb of the tides.

One of the lessons of a pilgrimage, indeed of life itself, is that the ebb tides are to be embraced, and even the worst will pass. Hard, though, to relax into those times of waning.

## Forty-nine

## Silence

The relation between us was
silence; that and the feeling
of each one being watched
by the other: I by an
enormous pupil in a blank
face, he by one in a million
wanderers in the darkness
that was never a long way off
from his presence.
                    It had begun
by my talking all of the time
repeating the worn formulae
of the churches in the belief
that was prayer. Why does silence
suggest disapproval? The prattling
ceased, not suddenly, but,
as flowers die off in a frost
my requests thinned. I contented
myself I was answering
his deafness with my dumbness. My tongue
lolled, clapper of a disused
bell that would never again
pound on him.
                    What are the emotions
of God? There was no admiring
of my restraint, no suggestion even
of a recompense for my patience.
If he had allowed himself but one
word: his name, for instance, spoken
ever so obliquely; my own that,
for all his majesty, acknowledged
my existence.
                    And yet there were creatures
around me with their ears
pricked; figures on ancient cathedrals,
the denizens of art, with their rapt,
innocent faces and heads on one side
as though they were listening. Ah, but to whom?

From *No truce with the Furies*, 1995
*Collected later poems*, p.287

Standing in an ancient church and remembering the sheer volume of words said and sung over the years, and pondering the silence that the walls enclose – as well as the silence that falls upon those words that no longer carry meaning for us.

On any journey, with any companion, the time comes when there are no more words. The rhythms of footsteps, of prayers and poems and hymns repeated, fade into the background, and we are oblivious to them even if we can still hear them: we are entering a deeper silence, perhaps a necessary one, towards the emerging of new language. But it will come only in the deepest silence of the night, the embraced silence of the poet who knows he must not speak now, not for years, and remain loyal to the silence of the desert places, outside and within.

Tony Brown writes this in the New Welsh Review: 'On so many occasions in the later poems the words reach beyond the boundaries of speech to where experience defeats, or transcends language, to the darkness and the silence where God may be ...'

**Fifty**

*Arrival*

Not conscious
    that you have been seeking
        suddenly
    you come upon it

the village in the Welsh hills
        dust free
    with no road out
but the one you came in by.

        A bird chimes
    from a green tree
the hour that is no hour
    you know. The river dawdles
to hold a mirror for you
where you may see yourself
    as you are, a traveller
        with the moon's halo
    above him, who has arrived
    after long journeying where he
        began, catching this
    one truth by surprise
that there is everything to look forward to.

From *Later poems*, 1983
*Collected poems*, p.427

Thinking of a railway station at the end of a line, or the source of a river at the end of a long walk upstream, or turning off a car engine at the end of a tiring journey.

A sigh of contentment. And even at the end of the journey there is 'everything to look forward to'.

## Fifty-one

### *'I think that maybe'*

I think that maybe
I will be a little surer
of being a little nearer.
That's all. Eternity
is in the understanding
that that little is more than enough.

From 'AD' in *Counterpoint*, 1990
*Collected later poems*, p.131

For a poet of place and location like R.S. Thomas, it is unusual to be able to suggest, for this poem, to read it 'anywhere, any time'.

John Pikoulis writes in the New Welsh Review: 'His late verses ... are universal in character and import. He speaks quietly, intently, in them using the simplest language and sounding their compressed phrases subtly to the inner ear in an act of the truthfullest telling ...'

Any other comment is superfluous.

## Fifty-two

### Evening

The archer with time
as his arrow – has he broken
his strings that the rainbow
is so quiet over our village?

Let us stand, then, in the interval
of our wounding, till the silence
turn golden and love is
a moment eternally overflowing.

From *No truce with the Furies*, 1995
*Collected later poems*, p.223

Recalling the bow of an archer and the rainbow in the sky, playing with the images, and looking at a watch and thinking of clock time as an arrow.

M. Wynn Thomas wrote in the New Welsh Review that R.S.Thomas had said that this was 'the one late poem he still cherished as his own.' Read the second stanza in a church, a place of silence and stillness, of waiting, yet of consolation, so that, as we pause on our lifelong pilgrimage, we may be encouraged and strengthened by an interval, where the wounds of the past may, if not healed, glow with a 'strange light' (see 'Groping'), and the wounds of the future anticipated without flinching, the final hollowing out into nothing being the necessary prelude to everything.

# THE QUESTIONS

There are questions we are the solution
to, others whose echoes we must expand
to contain.

From 'Emerging'; see p. xx

## From *Collected poems*

### From *The stones of the field*, 1946
17 questions, among them these two:

(On looking at a man working in the fields)

Ransack your brainbox, pull out the drawers
that rot in your heart's dust, and what have you to give
to enrich his spirit or the way he lives?

From 'Affinity'

(On the death of a father, asking of the son)

Did he rebuild out of the ragged embers
a new life, tempered to the sting of sorrow?

From 'The airy tomb'

### From *An acre of land*, 1952
11 questions, among them these two:

When spring wakens the hearts
of the young children to sing, what song shall be theirs?

From 'The old language'

Did the earth help them, time befriend
these last survivors? Did the spring grass
heal winter's ravages?

From 'Depopulation of the hills'

**From *The minister*, 1953**
16 questions, among them these two:


Did you dream, wanderer in the night,
of the ruined house with the one light
shining; and that you were the moth
drawn relentlessly out of the dark?


(On the stars)

And we who see them, where have we been
since last their splendour inflamed our mind
with huge questions not to be borne?


**From *Song at the year's turning*, 1955**
9 questions, none quoted here.


**From *Poetry for supper*, 1958**
24 questions, none quoted here.


**From *Tares*, 1961**
18 questions, among them these five:


(On pondering why he remembers a day in Abersoch)

Was it just that the girl smiled,
though not at me, and the men smoking
had the look of those who have come safely home?

From 'Abersoch'


(To the Welsh farmer of many of his earlier poems,
Prytherch)
Can't you see
behind the smile on the times' face
the cold brain of the machine
that will destroy you and your race?

From 'Too late'

(Putting words into the mouth of another who worked
on the land, Job Davies)

What's living but courage?

From 'Lore'


                    Am I the keeper
of the heart's relics, blowing the dust
in my own eyes?

From 'A Welsh testament'


Why, then, are my hands red
with the blood of so many dead?
Is this where I was misled?

Why are my hands this way
that they will not do as I say?
Does no God hear when I pray?

From 'Here'


**From *The bread of truth*, 1963**
     22 questions, among them these nine:

What have they come here to mourn?
...
What are these red faces for?
This incidence of pious catarrh
at the grave's edge?

From 'Funeral'


(On a tramp asking for tea)

Strong for a poor man
on his way – where?
...
Are his dreams rich?

From 'Tramp'


(On a husband and wife, millers)

Had a seed of love,
left from the threshing,
found a crack in their hearts?

From 'The mill'

(On Prytherch)

        Is truth so bare,
so dark, so dumb, as on your hearth
and in your company I found it?
Is not the evolving print of the sky
to be read, too; the mineral
of the mind worked? Is not truth choice,
with a clear eye and a free hand,
from life's bounty?

From 'Servant'


## From *Pieta,* 1966
        22 questions, among them these six:

        Sometimes they meet
in the high air; what is engendered
at contact?

From 'Swifts'


I have a desire to walk on the shore,
to visit the caged beast whose murmurings
kept me awake. What does it mean
that I have the power to do this
all day long, if I wish to?

        Have I been wise
in the past, letting my nostrils
plan my day? That salt scrubbing
left me unclean. Am I wise now,
with all this pain in the air,
to keep my room, reading perhaps
of that Being whose will is our peace?

From 'Within sound of the sea'


        What is a man's
price?

From 'There'

Often I try
to analyse the quality
of its silences. Is this where God hides
from my searching?

From 'In church'

## From *Not that he brought flowers,* 1968
    19 questions, among them these four:

    What is it drives a people
to the rejection of a great
Spirit, and after to think it returns
reconciled to the shroud
prepared for it?

From 'A grave unvisited'

        That gentleness
of green nature, reflected
in its people – what has one done
to deserve it?

From 'The green isle'

(On seeing a town's houses by the sea)
    Who first began
that refuse: time's waste
growing at the edge
of the clean sea?

From 'Sailors' hospital'

    How do I serve so
this being they have shut out
of their houses, their thoughts, their lives?

From 'They'

## From *H'm,* 1972
    10 questions, none quoted here.

## From *Young and old,* 1972
    2 questions, none quoted here.

**From *What is a Welshman?* 1974**
4 questions, none quoted here.


**From *Laboratories of the spirit*, 1975**
41 questions, 7 quoted here:

Not as in the old days I pray,
God. My life is not what it was.
Yours, too, accepts the presence of
the machine?

From 'Emerging'


What is the hand
for? The immaculate conception
preceding the delivery
of the first tool?

From 'The hand'


And the germs
swarmed, their alphabet
lengthened; where was the tongue
to pronounce it?

From 'The tool'


There is no defence
against laughter issuing
at the wrong time, but is there ever
forgiveness?

From 'Pardon'


What
is the serenity of art
worth without the angels
at the hot gates, whose sword
is time and our uneasy conscience?

From 'Now'


But the financiers will ask
in that day: Is it not better
to leave broken bank balances
behind us than broken heads?

From 'The interrogation'

**From *The way of it,* 1977**
   21 questions, 4 quoted here:


   What was his life
worth? Was there a tree he did not eat
of, because he was not tempted
to? And must we praise him for it?

From 'The valley dweller'


   And this life
that we lead, will it sound
well on the future's
cassette?

From 'Eheu! Fugaces'


   Whose silence so eloquent
as his? What word so explosive
as that one Palestinian
word with the endlessness of its fall-out?

From 'Nuclear'


Have I been too long on my knees
worrying over the obscurity
of a message?

From 'They'


**From *Frequencies* 1978**
   38 questions, 13 quoted here:


        And so I listen
instead and hear the language
of silence, the sentence
without an end. Is it I, then,
who am being addressed?

From 'Shadows'


   He will not come any more
to our lure. Why, then, do I kneel still
striking my prayers on a stone
heart? Is it in hope
one of them will ignite yet and throw
on its illumined walls the shadow
of someone greater than I can understand?

From 'The empty church'

To learn to distrust the distrust
of feeling – this then was the next step
for the seeker? To suffer himself to be persuaded
of intentions in being other than the crossing
of a receding boundary which did not exist?
To yield to an unfelt presence that, irresistible
in itself, had the character of everything
but coercion? To believe, looking up
into invisible eyes shielded against love's
glare, in the ubiquity of a vast concern?

From 'Perhaps'


What resources have I
other than the emptiness without him of my whole
being, a vacuum he may not abhor?

From 'The absence'


Is there a place
here for the spirit? Is there time
on this brief platform for anything
other than mind's failure to explain itself?

From 'Balance'


There
is no body in the stained window
of the sky now. Am I too late?
Were they too late also, those
first pilgrims? He is such a fast
God, always before us and
leaving as we arrive…

…Was the pilgrimage
I made to come to my own
self, to learn that in times
like these and for one like me
God will never be plain and
out there, but dark rather and
inexplicable, as though he were in here?

From 'Pilgrimages'

## From *Between here and now*, 1981
32 questions, 4 quoted here:

The tower
is a finger pointing
   up, but at whom?
            From 'Gauguin, Breton village in the snow'


In this desert of language
      we find ourselves in,
with the sign-post with the word 'God'
      worn away
                  and the distance...?
                        From 'Directions'


   When will he return
from his human exile, and will
peace then be restored
   to the flesh?

                        From 'Covenant'


      Divided
mind, the message is always
in two parts. Must it be
on a cross it is made one?

                        From 'Voices'


## From *Later poems*, 1983
31 questions, 11 quoted here:

   What was a sailor
good for who had sailed
all seas and learned wisdom
from none, fetched up there
in the shallows with his mind's
valueless cargo?
...
      And I,
can I accept your voyages
are done; that there is no tide
high enough to float you off
this mean shoal of plastic
and trash? Six feet down,
and the bone's anchor too
heavy for your child spirit
to haul on and be up and away?

                        From 'Salt'

    As the sun comes up
fresh, what is the darkness
stretching from the horizon
to horizon? It is the shadow
here of the forked man.
...
Summer is
at an end. The migrants
depart. When they return
in spring to the garden,
will there be a man among them?

From 'Thirteen blackbirds look at a man'


Is absence enough?
I asked from my absent place
by love's fire. What god,
fingers in its ears, leered at me
from above the lintel, face
worn by the lapping
of too much time? Leaves prompted
to prayer, green hands folded
in green evenings. Who
to? I questioned, avoiding
that chipped gaze. Was lightning
the answer, scissoring
between clouds, the divine
cut-out with his veins
on fire?

From 'Cadenza'


So God is born
        from our loss of nerve?

From 'The tree'


You refer to the fading away
of our prayers. May we suggest
you try listening instead on the inter-galactic
channel?

From 'Publicity Inc.'

**From *Ingrowing thoughts*, 1985**
> 3 questions, 1 quoted here:

What but genius can re-assemble
    the bones' jigsaw?

From 'Guernica: Pablo Picasso'


**From *Destinations*, 1985**
> 11 questions, 5 quoted here:

A message from God
delivered by a bird
at my window, offering friendship.
Listen. Such language!
Who said God was without
speech?

From 'The message'


Were there currents between them?
Why, when he thought darkly,
would the nerves play
at her lips' brim? What was the heart's depth?
There were fathoms in her,
too, and sometimes he crossed
them and landed and was not repulsed.

From 'He and she'


    What certainties
have I to hand on
like the punctuality

with which, at the moon's
rising, the bay breaks
into a smile, as though meaning
were not the difficulty at all?

From 'Sarn Rhiw'

**From *Welsh airs*, 1987**
 17 questions, 11 quoted here:

Where is our poetry
but in the footnotes?
What laurels for famous
men but asterisks and numbers?

From 'Dead worthies'


Ah, Jerusalem, Jerusalem!
Is it for nothing our chapels were christened
with Hebrew names? The Book rusts
in the empty pulpits above empty
pews, but the Word ticks inside
remorselessly as the bomb that is timed soon to go off.

From 'Waiting'


              What was sin
but the felix culpa enabling
a daughter of the soil to move
in divine circles?
...
Three pilgrimages to Bardsey
equalling one to Rome – How close
need a shrine be to be too far
for the traveller of today who is in
a hurry? Spare an hour or two
for Dolanog – no stone cross,
no Holy Father. What question
has the country to ask, looking as if
nothing has happened since the earth
cooled? And what is your question?
She was young and was taken.
If one asked you: 'Are you glad
to have been born? would you let
the positivist reply for you
by putting your car in gear, or watch
the exuberance of nature in a lost
village, that is life saying Amen
to itself? Here for a few years
the spirit sang on a bone bough
at eternity's window, the flesh trembling
at the splendour of a forgiveness
too impossible to believe in, yet believing.

Are the Amens over? Ann (Gymraeg)
you have gone now but left us with the question
that has a child's simplicity and a child's depth:
Does the one who called you

when the tree was green, call us
also if with changed voice,
now the leaves have fallen and the boughs
are of plastic, to the same thing?

From 'Fugue for Ann Griffiths'


## From *Experimenting with an Amen*, 1986
90 questions, 28 quoted here:

What
is perfection? Anonymity's
patent? A frame fitted
for effortless success
in conveying viruses
to the curved nostril?

From 'The Fly'


Who was it said: Fear
not, when fear is an ingredient
of our knowledge of you?

From 'Hebrews 12.29'


A wood.
A man entered;
thought he knew the way
through. The old furies
attended. Did he emerge
in his right mind? The same
man? How many years
passed? Aeons? What is
the right mind? What does
'same' mean? No change of clothes
for the furies?
...
Is it the self
that he mislaid? Is it why
he entered, ignoring
the warning of the labyrinth
without end? How many times
over must he begin again?

From 'The wood'

*123*

So the catechism begins:
'Who are you?'
                    'I don't know.'
'Who gave you that ignorance?'
'It is the system that, when two people
meet, they combine to produce
the darkness in which the self
is born, a wick hungering
for its attendant flame.'
                              'What will that
do for you?
                    'Do for me? It is the echo
of a promise I am meant
to believe in.'
...
                    'Life's simpleton,
know this gulf you have created
can be crossed by prayer. Let me hear
if you can walk it.'
                              'I have walked it.
It is called silence, and is a rope
                    over an unfathomable
abyss, which goes on and on
never arriving.'

                                        From 'Revision'


What power shall minister to us
at the closure of the century,
of the millennia? The god,
who was Janus-faced, is eclipsed
totally by our planet, by the shadow
cast on him by contemporary
mind. Shall we continue worshipping
that mind for its halo,
its light the mirage of its radiation?

                                        From 'AD2000'


        Is there a far side
to an abyss, and can our wings
take us there? Or is man's
meaning in the keeping of himself
afloat over seventy thousand
fathoms, tacking against winds
coming from no direction,
going in no direction?

                                        From 'Strands'

Ah, vertical God,
whose altitudes are the mathematics
        that confound us,
what is thought but mind's
        scream as it hurtles
in free-fall down your immense
side, hurrying everywhere,
arriving nowhere but at the precipitousness
        of your presence?

                                        From 'The cast'


        Before what cradle
                do the travellers from afar,
strontium and plutonium, hold out
                their thin gifts?
...

        What anthem have our computers
        to insert into the vacuum
by the break in transmission
        of the song upon Patmos?

                                        From 'Reply'


            And the mind,
then, weary of the pilgrimages
to its horizons – is there no spring of thought
adjacent to it, where it can be
dipped, so that emerging but
once in ten thousand times,
freed of its crutches, is sufficient
testimony to the presence in it
of a power other than its own?

                                        From 'Cures'



**From *Echoes return slow*, 1988**
        33 questions, 2 quoted here:

Does God listen
to them, crouched as he is
over the interminable problem
of how not to cheat, when the hell-born
spirit appears to be winning?

                (With a contemporary congregation in mind's eye,
                        the poem itself untitled.)

Have I been brought here

to repent of my sermons,
to erect silence's stone over
my remains, and to learn

from the lichen's slowness
at work something of the slowness
of the illumination of the self?

> (The poet in retirement, looking at the sea,
> the poem itself untitled.)


## From *Counterpoint*, 1990
42 questions, 6 quoted here:

Looking at it
without seeing it.
Is this the secret
of life, the masked ball

which meaning attends
incognito, as once men looked
in a manger, failing
to see the beast for the god?

> (From the sequence entitled 'Incarnation',
> the poem itself untitled.)


What are the stars
but time's fires going out
before ever the crucified
can be taken down?

> (From the sequence entitled 'Crucifixion',
> the poem itself untitled.)


Was there a mathematics
before matter to which
you were committed? Or is it
man's mind is to blame,
spinning questions out of itself
in the infinite regress?

> From the sequence entitled 'Crucifixion',
> the poem itself untitled.)

Darkness arrived at
midday, the shadow
of whose wing?

(From the sequence entitled 'Crucifixion',<br>the poem itself untitled.)


Nothing is outside
God. We have attributed
violence to him. Why not
implicate him in injections?

(From the sequence entitled 'AD',<br>the poem itself untitled.)


**From *Mass for hard times,* 1992**
85 questions, 26 quoted here:


(What has physics to do
with the heart's need?) Am I
too late, then, with my language?
Are symbols to be in future
the credentials of our approach?
(And how contemporary
is the Cross, that long-bow drawn
against love?) My questions
accumulate in the knowledge
it is words are the kiss of Judas
that must betray you.

From 'Mass for hard times: Credo'


No longer the Lamb
but the idea of it.
Can an idea bleed?
On what altar
does one sacrifice an idea?

From 'Mass for hard times: Agnus Dei'

What
does the traveller to your door
ask, but that you sit down
and share with him that
for which there are no words?

From 'One day'


How will the lion remain a lion
if it eat straw like the ox?

Where will the little child lead them
who has not been there before?

From 'Questions to the prophet'


Of whom
does the scarecrow remind,
arms wide as though pierced

by the rain's nails, while
the motorist goes by insolently
wagging his speedometer's finger?

From 'Come down'


Shall we revise the language?
And in revising the language
will we alter the doctrine?

Do we seek to plug the hole
in faith with faith's substitute
grammar? And are we to be saved

by translation?

From 'Bleak liturgies'


Where to turn? To whom
to appeal? The prayer probes
have been launched and silence
closes behind them? The Amens
are rents in the worn fabric
of meaning. Are we
our own answer? Is
to grow up to destroy
childhood's painting of one
who was nothing but vocabulary's

shadow? Where do the stone
faces come from but from
trying to meet the sky's
empty stare?

From 'Bleak liturgies'


    We are so long
in dying – time granted
to discover a purpose
in our decay?

From 'The Seasons: Autumn'


      'Are you there?'
I call into the dumb
past, that is close to me
as my shadow.
      'Are you here?'
I whisper to the encountered
self like one coming
on the truth asleep
and fearing to disturb it.

From 'Pen Llŷn'


      What genealogy
has the self other
than the wisdom gathered
from standing so often
before time's firing
squad, computing its
eternity in the triggered interval
before the command to shoot?

From 'Jaromir Hladik'


You chose the natural timber
to die on that the natural
man should be saved. What boughs,
then, will need to be crossed
and what body crucified
upon them for salvation
to be won for the astronauts
venturing in their air-conditioned
capsules? Will artificial living
give birth to the artificial
sin? What prayers will they say
upside down in their space-chambers?

*129*

Are you prepared to reveal
the nuclear brain and the asbestos
countenance to deserve their worship?
They are planning their new conurbations
a little nearer the stars,
incinerated by day and by night
glacial; but will there be room there
for a garden for the Judas
of the future to make his way through
to give you his irradiated kiss?

From 'What then?'


**From *No truce with the furies*, 1995**
    96 questions, 18 quoted here:


            Is prayer
not a glass that, beginning
in obscurity as his books
do, the longer we stare
into the clearer becomes
the reflection of a countenance
in it other than our own?

From 'S.K.'


Where is that place apart
you summon us to? Noisily
we seek it and have no time
to stay. Stars are distant;
is it more distant still,
out in the dark in the shadow
of thought itself?

From 'Wrong?'


What do whales say
calling to one another
on their extended wave-lengths?
...

            Their immense
brain cannot save them;
can ours, launching us
into fathomless altitudes, save us?

From 'No Jonahs'

What are the leaves in autumn
but the mind flaking beneath
truth's chisel?

From 'Incarnations'


       Beasts walk
among birds and never
do the birds scare; but the human,
that alienating shadow
with the Bible under the one
arm and under the other
the bomb, as often
drawn as he is repelled
by the stranger waiting for him
in the mirror – how
can he return home
when his gaze forages
beyond the stars? Pity him,
then, this winged god, rupturer
of gravity's control
accelerating on and
outward in the afterglow
of a receding laughter?

From 'Winged god'


       What love sentenced
us to murder in order
that we survive? Does God know
what it is to eat his food
off the ground, to draw sustenance
from intestines?

From 'The Mass of Christ'


Is it our music interprets you
best, a heart-beat at the very centre
of your creation? Is it art,
depicting man's figure as the conductor
to your lightning?

From 'Neither'


Our experiments are repeatable,
but what is love the precipitate
of? We have eaten of a tree
whose foliage is radioactive

and the autumn of
its fall-out is upon our children.

Why, then, of all possible
turnings do we take
this one rather than that,
when the only signs discernible
are what no one has erected?
Is it because, at the road's
ending, the one who is as a power
in hiding is waiting to be christened?

From 'The waiting'


     What, as a composer,
could I do but mimic

its deciduous notes
flaking from it
with a feather's softness
but as frigidly as snow?

From 'Barn owl'


     Why does silence
suggest disapproval?

From 'Silence'


Windy and wet, and what is
worse the weather within
wicked: wounds and the heart's
woe, when all should be well.
Ah, waif spirit, will you not wake
once again to wonder and worship?

From 'Anybody's alphabet'


**From _Residues_, 2002**
    42 questions, 5 quoted here:

     How many men
have leaned, spat, dreamed
by a fire, remembering love,
youth, victory, happier
times, and the uselessness of remembering?

From 'Dreaming'

Are the machine and the tiger
related by more than a purr?

From 'Contradictions'

Do we put too much
on? Is the self there
so pared down as to be
invisible as glass?

From 'Finality'

Could we have known
that back of their faces hope
ticked to alternative rhythms;
that within the arteries
of the state itself the anti-coagulating
influences were at work?

From 'Prague spring'

# COUNTERPOINT

# QUESTIONS FROM THE GOSPELS

There are many more questions, some incidental, some implied. This is a selection of those worth pondering, not least on a pilgrim journey.

Jesus's parables and sayings in themselves raise questions, and would have divided opinion among his hearers. He likened the Kingdom of God (Matthew substitutes 'heaven' to avoid naming God to his Jewish audience) to all kinds of unexpected people and things, and, as John Dominic Crossan points out, there is an implied question: And how is the Kingdom of God like that? He doesn't give the answer himself.

With the occasional nod to the AV/KJV in its 400th anniversary year.

Did you not know that I must be about my Father's business?

*Luke 2.49*


There's more to life than food and clothing, isn't there?

*Matthew 6.25*


Can any of you add one hour to your life or one centimetre to your height by fretting about it?

*Matthew 6.27*


Why do you notice the speck of dust in your friend's eye, but overlook the plank in your own?

*Matthew 7.3*


Why are you such cowards, you with your meagre trust, 'O ye of little faith'?

*Matthew 8.26*


Who is my mother? And who are my brothers and sisters?

*Matthew 12.48*


Why do you break God's commandment because of your tradition?

*Matthew 15.3*


What about you, who do you say I am?

*Matthew 16.15*


What good will it do you if your acquire the whole world but forfeit your life?

*Matthew 16.26*


Wasn't it only fair for you to treat your fellow slave with the same consideration as I treated you? What a huge debt I forgave you, what a small debt you refused to forgive!

*Matthew 18.33*


What do you want me to do for you?

*Matthew 20.32*

What is your name? What is its meaning?

*Mark 5.9*


Do you not perceive? Do you not understand? Have you hardened
your hearts? You have eyes, do you not see? You have ears, do you
not hear? Do you not remember?

*Mark 8.17–18*


Can the blind lead the blind? Will they not both fall into the ditch?

*Luke 6.39*


Why do you call me 'Master', and do not do the things which I tell
you?

*Luke 6.46*


Which of these three, the priest, the Levite, or the Samaritan was a
neighbour to the man who fell into the hands of the thieves?

*Luke 10.36*


If I have told you earthly things, and you do not believe, how will you
believe if I tell you of heavenly things?

*John 3.12*


You have been paralyzed for so long. Do you really want to be
healed?

*John 5.6*


Will you also drift away from me?

*John 6.67*


Everyone who is alive and believes in me will never die. Do you
believe this?

*John 11.26*


In washing your feet, do you really understand what I have done for
you?

*John 13.12*


Can you drink the cup that I am about to drink?

*Matthew 20.22*

What, couldn't you stay awake with me for one hour? Keep
awake; watch.

*Matthew 26.40*


Judas, do you betray the Truly Human One ('the Son of Man')
with a kiss?

*Luke 22.48*


My God, my God, why have you abandoned me?

*Matthew 27.46*


Why do you seek the living among the dead?

*Luke 24.5*


Why are you disturbed? Why are your minds bewildered?

*Luke 24.38*


*Three times denying, three times questioned:*

Do you love me more than the others do? ...
Do you love me? ...
Are you my friend? ...

*Each reply in a lower quieter voice, with no pause in answering the first
question, and a long pause in answering the third. And only then is he at
last in truth.*

*John 21.15–17*